PAINTED LADIES

Corbels &
Gingerbread

Robert and Lynn Gatchell

Schiffer Publishing Ltd

4880 Lower Valley Road, Atglen, PA 19310

Other Schiffer Books by Robert and Lynn Gatchell
Painted Ladies: Balusters & Columns, 978-0-7643-3045-2, $29.99

Other Schiffer Books on Related Subjects
Gingerbread Gems: Victorian Architecture of Oak Bluffs, 978-0-7643-2682-0, $29.95
Gingerbread Gems: Victorian Architecture of Cape May, 0-7643-1971-X
Architectural Details from Victorian Homes, 0-7643-1829-2, $49.95

Schiffer Books are available at special discounts for bulk purchases for sales promotions or premiums. Special editions, including personalized covers, corporate imprints, and excerpts can be created in large quantities for special needs. For more information contact the publisher:

Published by Schiffer Publishing Ltd.
4880 Lower Valley Road
Atglen, PA 19310
Phone: (610) 593-1777; Fax: (610) 593-2002
E-mail: Info@schifferbooks.com

Please visit our web site catalog at www.schifferbooks.com

We are always looking for people to write books on new and related subjects. If you have an idea for a book please contact us at the above address.

This book may be purchased from the publisher.
Include $5.00 for shipping.
Please try your bookstore first.
You may write for a free catalog.

In Europe, Schiffer books are distributed by
Bushwood Books
6 Marksbury Ave.
Kew Gardens
Surrey TW9 4JF England
Phone: 44 (0) 20 8392-8585; Fax: 44 (0) 20 8392-9876
E-mail: info@bushwoodbooks.co.uk
Website: www.bushwoodbooks.co.uk
Free postage in the U.K., Europe; air mail at cost.
Try your bookstore first.

Designed by RoS
Type set in New Baskerville BT

ISBN: 978-0-7643-3046-9
Printed in China

<u>1864</u>

Bigenuf

The Gatchell Family Home

1951- 1979

<u>Acknowledgment</u>

Thank you to all our friends and family, who encouraged us to publish our work. Thanks to all the friendly homeowners, who graciously allowed us close up access for the detail photos. Finally, special thanks to Ann and John Nelson, and Earl Jecoy for their guidance and support.

<u>Dedication</u>

For Kyle and Jennifer
Happiness Always

<u>1875</u>

Lavender & Old Lace

004

1879
Tabernacle

Preface

"This book is an excellent photographic library of Victorian architectural details. Architects, builders, and historic preservationists will find it useful for its details that can be used on new designs as well as renovations of historic homes. Regular homeowners will find the variety of images useful to decide what Victorian details to add to their own home."

Kyle S. Gatchell
Owner, KG Construction
Alumni, Roger Williams University,
School of Architecture

Builder's Poem
"Architecture"

Ah, to build, to build!
That is the noblest art of all the arts. Painting and sculpture are but images, are
merely shadows cast by outward things on stone or canvas, having in themselves no
separate existence. Architecture, existing in itself, and not in seeming a something it
is not, surpasses them as substance shadow.
Henry Wadsworth Longfellow

Contents

Introduction

Painted Ladies: Corbels and Gingerbread includes the homes located in the historical district of Oak Bluffs (Cottage City), Massachusetts: Ocean Park and several more that were moved from Martha's Vineyard's campgrounds to East Chop. The Martha's Vineyard Campgrounds are a cluster of over three hundred homes governed by the Martha's Vineyard Camp Meeting Association and often referred to as "The Campgrounds."

The Campground architecture is a hybrid of design adapted by island carpenters using available materials and technology. The origin of the island's completely native architecture is a unique blend of "Carpenter Gothic, Greek Revival and Victorian." At first, tents were erected in circles around the huge tent used by the Methodists for their great revival "camp meetings." The first homes created a true "tent city." These were followed by platforms as the tent-owners returned yearly, and more permanent walls and roofs were added. Gradually, the tents became small cottages, side-by-side in cozy Christian intimacy as if packed into rows at the prayer meetings. These permanent structures maintained the original footprint of the tents, which may explain the closeness of the homes and why some roofs are actually connected.

Many of the cottages have two front doors, like tent flaps, facing the narrow street. Some have pretty little verandas, or small fenced miniature gardens. Over the front door, many have balconies, with very high peaked roofs.

These cottage dwellers began to assert their individuality as they decorated, rimming the eaves and framing the porches with scroll and fretwork. The balconies, windows, and doors are decorated in scroll and fretwork, and sometimes stained glass. Rarely would gingerbread be put on the side or rear of the home — rather the embellishment was used as a grand accent. The cottage owners avoided having monotonous homes with imaginative use of trim and color. At every turn the homes are gaily painted in a rainbow of color. A little paint and gingerbread go a long way. Whimsy is added with the unique or descriptive names of the cottages. Some describe a sentiment, like "Open Door," size: "Small Fry," "Bigenuf," and "Tall Timber" or choice of color: "Oops."

Wealthy people building larger homes echoed the Campground cottage style while incorporating many of the European styles of the time. Gothic Revival was used from 1830 to 1870, followed by the Queen Ann style, which lasted to the turn of the century. A person could discern the wealth of the owners by the size of the home, and the amount and intricacy of the scroll and fretwork.

Gingerbread

The word Gingerbread has been used to describe the collective effects of the details adorning Victorian structures. Gingerbread, in general, refers to the carved or pierced wooden ornament (photo 256) often found on Victorian houses. A style was so named because of the resemblance to sugar-frosted decoration on gingerbread cookie houses. The work was usually hand-carved, wood turned on a lathe and/or fashioned on a jigsaw. This ornamentation flourished with the invention of the scroll saw. Gingerbread is designed to be simple (photo 502), lighthearted (photo 349), humorous (photo 292, "the hunter"), and colorful (photo 606 or 212). The more specific term "Gingerbread" (also known as verge board or bargeboard) refers to the highly decorative boards or other elaborate fretwork design (photo 021 or 174) pieces fixed to the edges of the gable roof (photo 038 or 603) or projecting rafters (photo 003). Many of the homes have multiple rooflines (photo 083 or 551) with varying roof pitches and this trim runs along the rooflines and/or the dormers, usually hanging perpendicular from the projecting edge of a roof gable. There are some homes, which repeat the same gingerbread in varying sizes on the home, while others will have different designs for the roofline and dormers (photo 023 or 108).

Corbels

Corbels (also called brackets) are often a triangular decorative (photo 151 or 041) or structure (upside-down L-shape) that projects from a wall (photo 020) or other vertical surface, and supports another component, such as an eave or balcony (photo 197). These ornamental corbel pieces are found under eaves (photo 030), ends of windowsills (photo 198 or 107), edge of posts (photo 185 or 285), or frame arches (photo 493). Some appear to provide structural support for overhangs (photo 197 or 051) or cantilevered projections (photo 335). Other corbels are just used for decorative effect; some will be simple curves (photo 092 or 189), some will have multiple layers (photo 113 or 210), while others will be constructed of intricate fretwork lattice (photo 172 or 221).

Eyebrows

Eyebrows are the decorative roof-like decorations found above windows and doors. They follow the arch of the structure and are often painted a contrasting color (photo 396) to enhance the embellishment. Many eyebrows will end with a turned finial, while others may end with small outward horizontal wings. The eyebrow shapes include: triangular arch (photo 209 or 572), Gothic arch (photo 344 or 567), rounded arch (photo 139), square top arch (photo 139 or 357), and steeple-like (photo 529). A few will look like very delicate lace-work (photo 124 or 504) or include mini gingerbread (photo 231).

The Homes & their
<u>Architectural Details</u>

001

<u>1977</u>
The Gatchell's

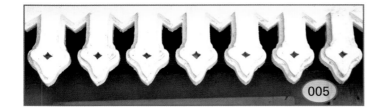

005

006

007

008

<u>1864</u>
1ST Cottage Built on the Camp Grounds

010

011

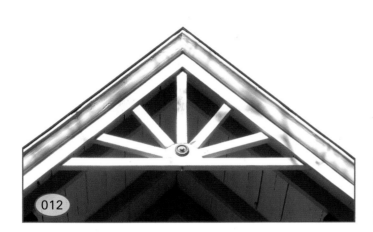

012

013

014

015

016

017

018

019

021

020

022

023

<u>1867</u>
Summer Love

026

027

028

024

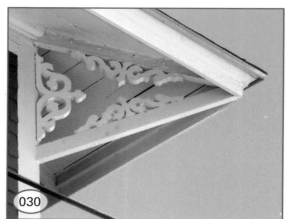

030

025

031

029

032

Purple Angel

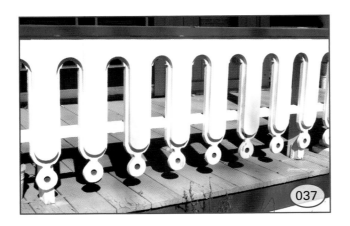

034

035

039

036

040

041

1867

Bell Buoy & Captain's Corner

049

UNITED
METHODIST
PARISH
HOUSE
SUNDAY
Church School 9:30am
Built 1886, Remodelled 1966
WELCOME
050

1886

Parish House

Remodeled in 1966

051

052

053

054

055

056

059

057

058

060

061

1867

Remodeled 2006
One of the few winterized homes

063

064

065

066

067

1870

Small Frey

070

071

068

073

072

074

075

076

1867

Coeup de L'isle

081

082

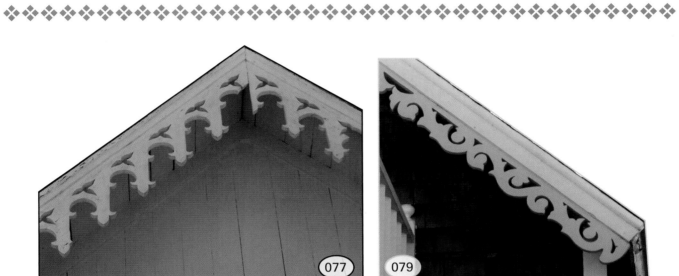

077

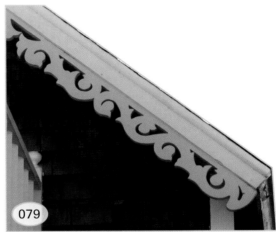

079

080

078

086

087

088

083

1867

084

085

089

090

091

092

094

093

095

096

098

097

099

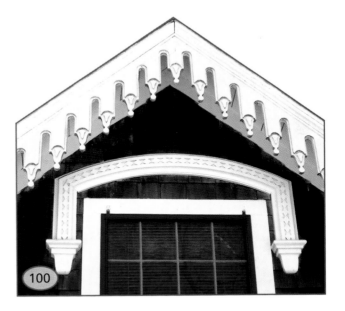

100

101

Keytokarma

108

1869

109

Victorian with Gambrel balcony roof

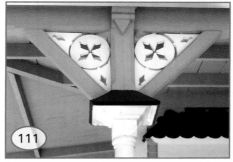

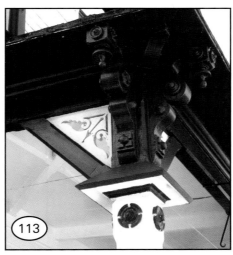

116

1869
The Bishop Gilbert Haven Cottage
Visited by President Grant in 1874

121

1870

Vineyard Magic

122

123

124

100

1867

125

126

127

128

129

130

131

132

133

142

Summer Time

143

144

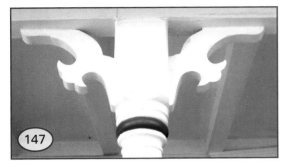

147

145

146

148

150

151

149

152

153

154

159

157

155

156

158

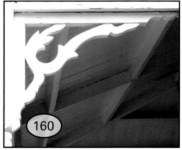

160

161

162

163

<u>1876</u>

Oops

164

165

166

167

169

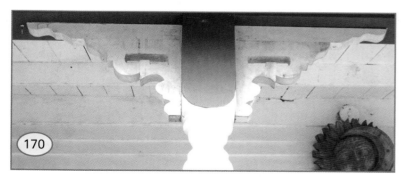

170

171

168

172

173

174

175

176

177

178

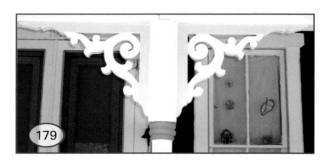

179

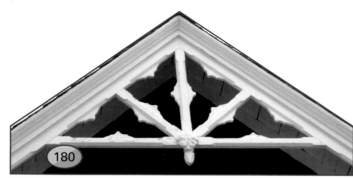

180

181

182

183

184

185

186

187

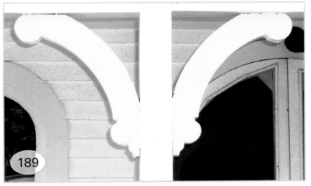

189

188

194

190

191

193

195

192

Nevadun

196

1876

Two neighbors displaying grand individuality

1869

224

225

226

227

228

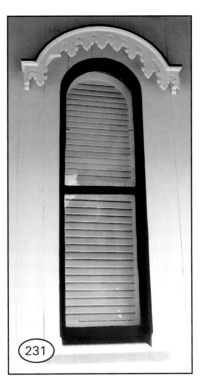

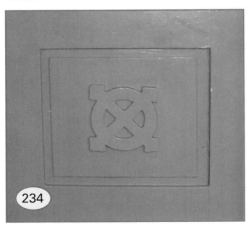

235

1867

Whitney Cottage

236

237

240

238

241

239

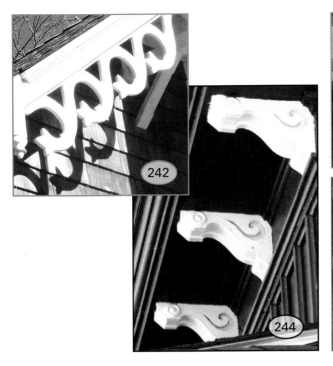

242

243

244

245

246

247

248

249

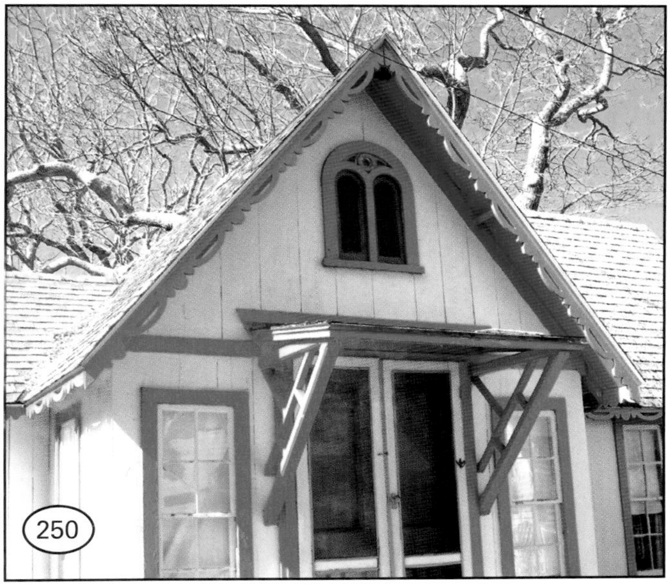
250

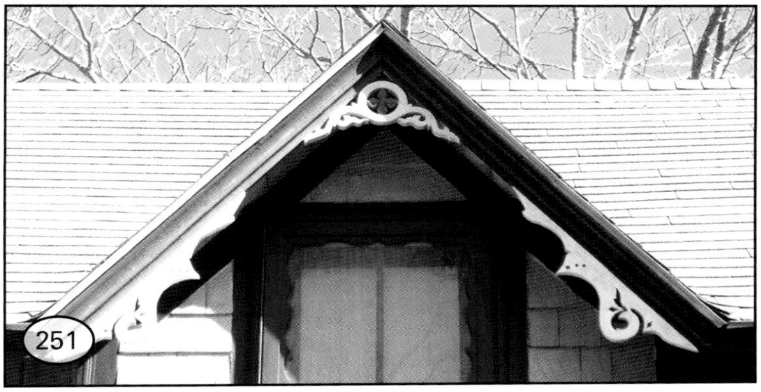
251

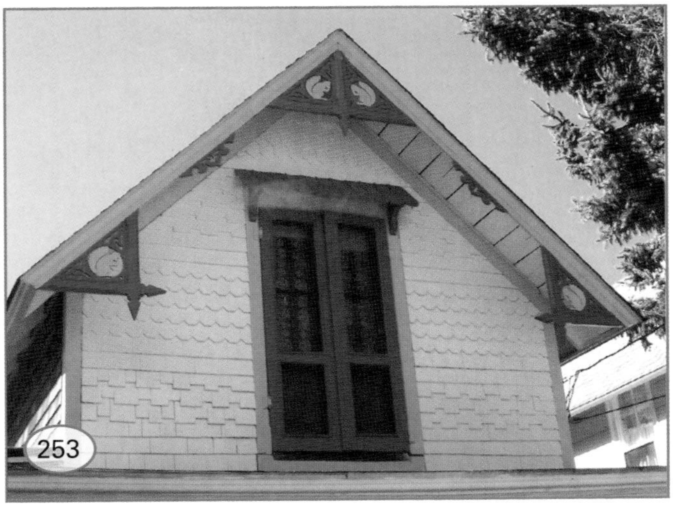
253

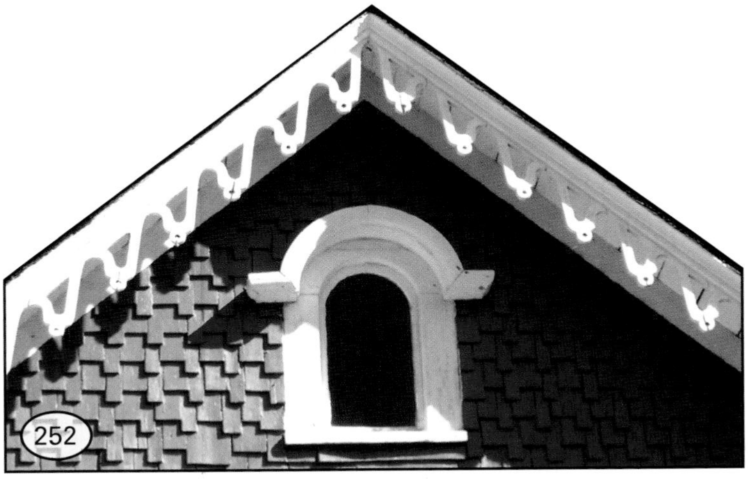
252

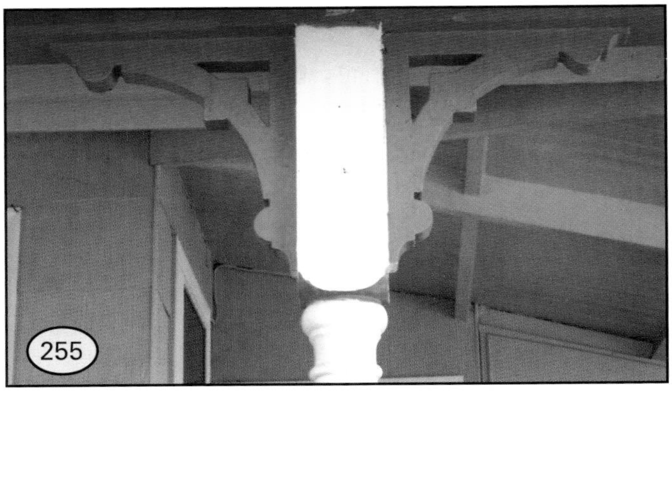
255

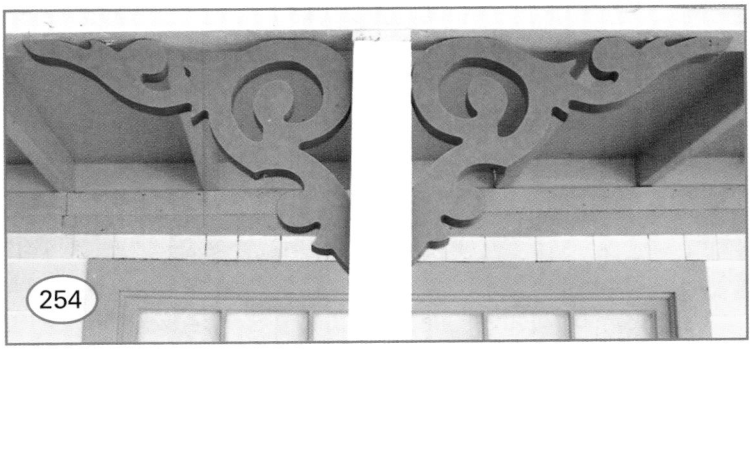
254

256

1870

257

258

259

260

261

263

1867
Looking Glass

262

1871

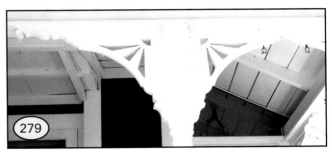

280

Koldkorner

281

282

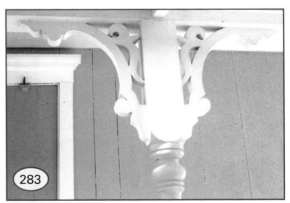

283

284

KOLDKORNER

285

287

286

289

288

290

291

Frost

292

Hunter House

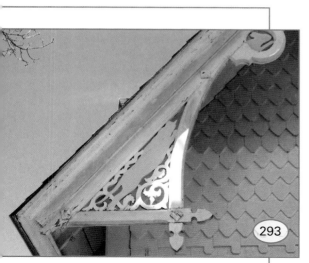

293

Dog chases the Rabbit

294

Rabbit and Hunter

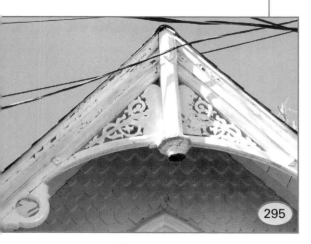

295

The Hunter

296

297

298

299

300

301

302

305

303

304

306

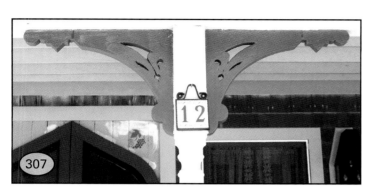

307

308

309

310

311

312

320

1868

Sea Shrimp

323

325

322

324

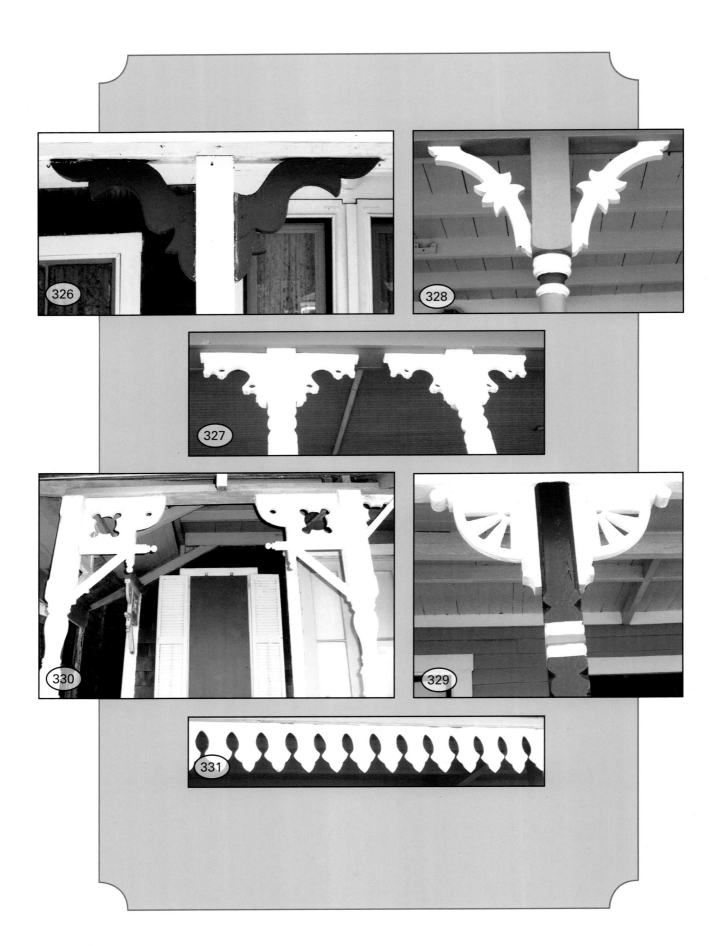

332

337

<u>1874</u>
Attleboro House

333

334

335

336

338

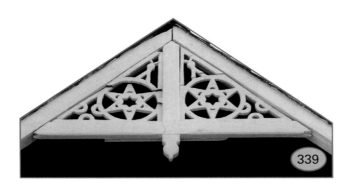

339

342

340

343

341

1870
La Verda Stello (The Green Star)

346

345

348

347

351

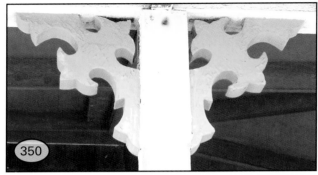

350

353

352

355

354

1876

Bittersweet

356

357

360

358

359

361

362

363

364

365

366

367

368

369

Tri-color roof home on Ocean Park

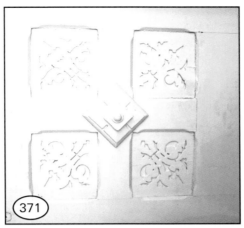

371

372

373

374

375

376

377

378

379

380

381

382

383

384

385

386

387

Petunia Patch

389

390

393

Classic Victorian

394

395

396

397

400

398

399

401

402

403

404

405

407

408

406

409

Summer time on Bayliss Avenue

420

419

421

422

423

424

425

426

428

427

435

436

437

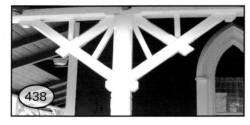

438

439

440

441

The Maxwell House

444

445

446

447

443

Crystal Place

448

451

450

452

449

453

455

463

458

456

459

464

462

460

461

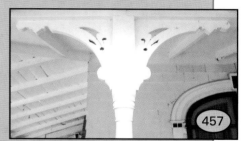

457

454

465

466

Lazy Days

469

467

468

471

470

472

473

474

475

476

477

478

Purple cottage with fretwork corbels

479

1872

486

487

1876

488

489

490

491

492

Balcony corbels accent the curved bracket

494

495

497

496

498

499

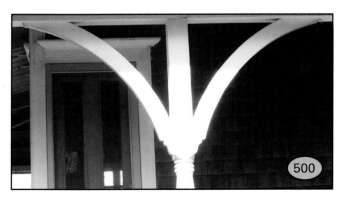

500

501

1867

Scotland's Yard

504

505

506

507

508

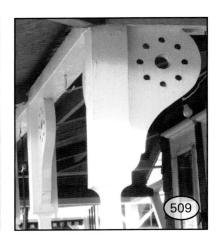

509

511

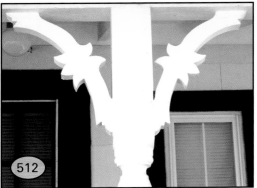

512

510

513

514

516

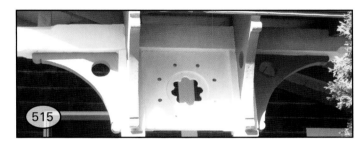

515

517

518

520

519

521

522

523

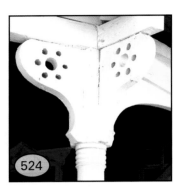

524

525

526

528

529

531

527

530

533

532

One of the last remaining cottages resembling a tent.

535

536

537

539

538

534

Ornate corbels and balusters compliment this Victorian home.

540

Ocean Park Gazebo

541

542

543

544

545

546

547

548

550

549

A PRIVATE HOME

1891
Corbin-Norton
Rebuilt in 2004

552

553

554

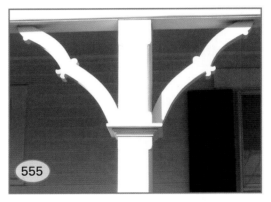

555

556

557

558

55 Ocean Park in full spring sun.

559

560

561

562

563

565

566

564

567

568

570

571

573

572

574

569

<u>1881</u>

Cinderella Cottage

575

579

576

577

578

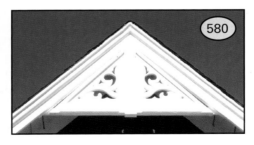

580

581

1890

585

584

582

583

586

587

588

589

592

591

590

Villa Rosa
African American Heritage Trail of Martha's Vineyard

594

595

597

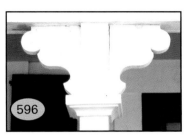

596

599

598

600

601

603

604

605

Tall Timber

606

<u>1867</u>

Greenup

Oak Bluffs

LEGEND

✳ PUBLIC REST ROOMS	★ POLICE DEPT	🏴 TOWN HALL	🚲 BIKE RACKS	$ CASH MACHINE/BANK
ⓘ INFORMATION	Ⓕ FIRE DEPT	Ⓛ LIBRARY	Ⓣ TAXI STAND	⛏ PUBLIC BEACHES
📮 POST OFFICE	✚ HOSPITAL	🚏 BUS STOP	⛴ FERRY	⛵ SMALL BOATING

OAK BLUFFS HARBOR

TO FALMOUTH

TO HYANNIS NANTUCKET

TO WOODS HOLE

EAST CHOP DRIVE

TO EAST CHOP LIGHTHOUSE

CROMWELL AVENUE

NEW YORK AVENUE

SACO AVENUE

PEQUOT AVE

SEAVIEW AVENUE EXT

CIRCUIT AVE

SUNSET LAKE

LAKE AVENUE

LAKE AVENUE

OAK BLUFFS AVENUE

TEMAHIGAN AVENUE

TOWANTICUT AVENUE

COMMONWEALTH

ROCK AVENUE

FOURTH AVENUE

COUNTY PARK

PARK AVENUE

CENTRAL

AVENUE

OCEAN AVENUE

PENNACOOK

PAWTICKET

ALLEN AVENUE

TRINITY PARK

MONTGOMERY AVE

TRINITY

NARRAGANSETT

OCEAN PARK

TRINITY PARK

BLOOM AVENUE

THE TABERNACLE

TRINITY PARK

SCHOOL STREET

HIGHLAND AVENUE

AVENUE

COTTAGE PARK

PARK AVENUE

GROVE AVENUE

SAMOSET

OCEAN AVENUE

NEW YORK

COUNTY

RURAL CIRCLE

MT HOPE AVE

PENNACOOK AVENUE

EASTVILLE AVENUE

ROCKIZ AVENUE

WASHINGTON PARK

CIRCUIT AVENUE

HARTFORD

MASSASOIT

PEQUOT

NARRAGANSETT

AVENUE

AVENUE

WEST CHURCH AVENUE

DUKES

CLINTON AVENUE

WASHINGTON

WABSUTTA AVENUE

TUCKERNUCK

NIANTIC AVENUE

WAMSUTTA AVENUE

PENNACOOK AVENUE

AVENUE

BEACH ROAD

VINEYARD AVE

LINCOLN AVENUE

AVENUE

NIANTIC PARK

TUCKERNUCK

WABAN PARK

HIAWATHA PARK

POLARNET

NASHAWENA

PARK

NANTUCKET AVENUE

MASONIC STREET

PEQUOT

VATAN

AVENUE

VIERA PARK

CANONICUS AVENUE

Ⓕ

KING ROAD

COUNTY RD

TRIANGLE

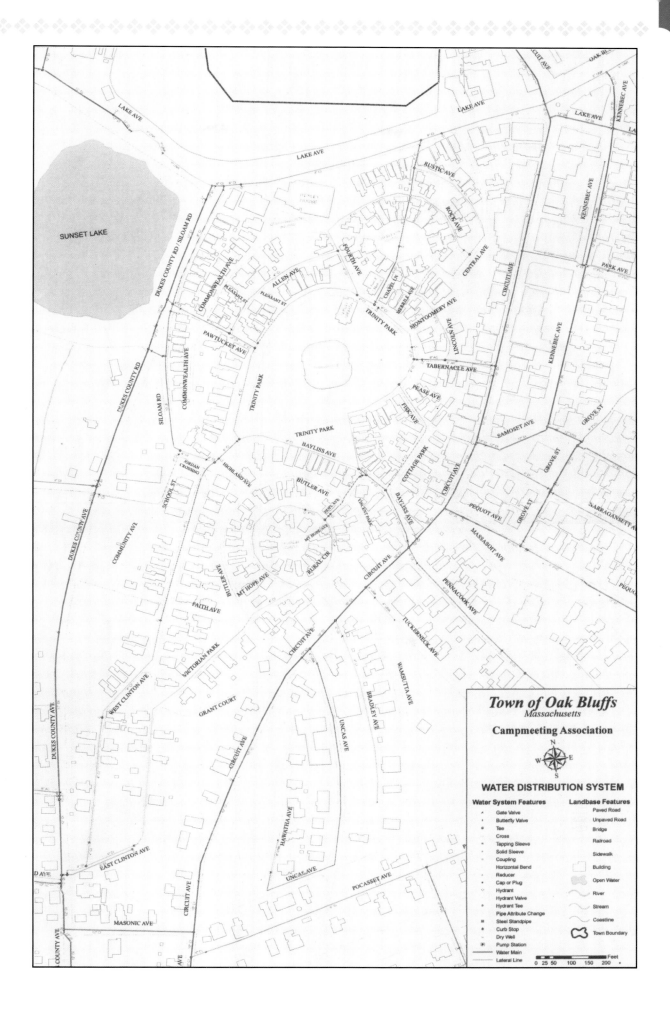

Photo Index

No.	No.	Location	Page
151	31	West Clinton Ave	45
152	24	West Clinton Ave	46
153	23	West Clinton Ave	46
154	23	West Clinton Ave	46
155	22	West Clinton Ave	46
156	22	West Clinton Ave	46
157	21	West Clinton Ave	46
158	21	West Clinton Ave	46
159	18	West Clinton Ave	46
160	16	West Clinton Ave	46
161	7	West Clinton Ave	46
162	49	Clinton Ave	46
163	57	Trinity Park	47
164	49	Clinton Ave	48
165	45	Clinton Ave	48
166	45	Clinton Ave	48
167	35	Clinton Ave	48
168	35	Clinton Ave	48
169	31	Clinton Ave	48
170	31	Clinton Ave	48
171	25	Clinton Ave	48
172	23	Clinton Ave	49
173	19	Clinton Ave	49
174	13	Clinton Ave	49
175	9	Clinton Ave	49
176	5	Clinton Ave	49
177	19	Victorian Park	49
178	16	Victorian Park	50
179	13	Victorian Park	50
180	13	Victorian Park	56
181	11	Victorian Park	50
182	8	Victorian Park	50
183	6	Victorian Park	50
184	6	Victorian Park	50
185	5	Victorian Park	50
186	3	Victorian Park	51
187	26	Victorian Park	51
188	24	Victorian Park	51
189	24	Victorian Park	51
190	22	Victorian Park	51
191	22	Victorian Park	51
192	27	Victorian Park	52
193	7	Butler Ave	51
194	7	Butler Ave	51
195	27	Victorian Park	52
196	28	Victorian Park	53
197	19	Butler Ave	54
198	19	Butler Ave	54
199	19	Butler Ave	54
200	19	Butler Ave	54
201	37	Butler Ave	54
202	39	Butler Ave	54
203	39	Butler Ave	54
204	76	Rural Circle	54
205		Mt Hope/ Rural Circle	55
206	15	Forest Circle	55
207	1	Forest Circle	55
208	1	Forest Circle	55
209	3	Forest Circle	55
210	3	Forest Circle	55
211	4	Forest Circle	55
212	10 & 11	Forest Circle	56
213	4	Forest Circle	58
214	4	Forest Circle	58
215	11	Forest Circle	58
216	13	Butler Ave	58
217		Dukes County Ave	58
218		Dukes County Ave	58
219	9	Dukes County Ave	58
220	69	Trinity Park	58
221	2	Bayliss Ave	59
222	2	Bayliss Ave	59
223	1	Bayliss Ave	59
224	6	Bayliss Ave	60
225	5	Bayliss Ave	60
226	9	Bayliss Ave	60
227	9	Bayliss Ave	60
228	11	Bayliss Ave	60
229	11	Bayliss Ave	61
230	11	Bayliss Ave	61
231	12	Bayliss Ave	61
232	1	Cottage Park	61
233	1	Cottage Park	61
234	1	Cottage Park	61
235	12	Cottage Park	62
236	2	Cottage Park	63
237	7	Cottage Park	63
238	8	Cottage Park	63
239	11	Cottage Park	63
240	12	Cottage Park	63
241	15	Cottage Park	63
242	16	Cottage Park	64
243	16	Cottage Park	64
244	6	Fisk Ave	64
245	8	Fisk Ave	64
246	8	Fisk Ave	64
247	14	Vincent Park	64
248	14	Vincent Park	64
249	7	Vincent Park	64
250	1	Pease Ave	65
251	8	Tabernacle Ave	65
252	5	Tabernacle Ave	65
253	2	Tabernacle Ave	65
254	2	Tabernacle Ave	65
255	1	Tabernacle Ave	65
256	16	Wesleyan Grove	66
257	1	Tabernacle Ave	67
258	47	Trinity Park	67
259	15	Wesleyan Grove	67
260	17	Wesleyan Grove	67
261	18	Wesleyan Grove	68
262	18	Wesleyan Grove	68
263	18	Wesleyan Grove	68
264	20	Wesleyan Grove	69
265	24	Wesleyan Grove	69
266	24	Wesleyan Grove	69
267	2	Wesleyan Grove	69
268	2	Wesleyan Grove	69
269	6	Wesleyan Grove	69
270	10	Wesleyan Grove	69
271	10	Wesleyan Grove	69
272	3	Chapel Lane	69
273	3	Chapel Lane	69
274	15	Fourth Ave	70
275	3	Chapel Lane	71
276	10	Fourth Ave	71
277	15	Fourth Ave	71
278	26	Allen Ave	71
279	26	Commonwealth Ave	71
280	24	Commonwealth Ave	72
281	24	Commonwealth Ave	73
282	24	Commonwealth Ave	73
283	24	Commonwealth Ave	73
284	24	Commonwealth Ave	73
285	18	Commonwealth Ave	74
286	18	Commonwealth Ave	74
287	21	Commonwealth Ave	74
288	21	Commonwealth Ave	74
289	21	Commonwealth Ave	74
290	14	Commonwealth Ave	74
291	53	Ocean Ave	75
292	17	Commonwealth Ave	76
293	17	Commonwealth Ave	77
294	17	Commonwealth Ave	77
295	17	Commonwealth Ave	77
296	17	Commonwealth Ave	77
297	12	Commonwealth Ave	77
298	10	Commonwealth Ave	77
299	7	Commonwealth Ave	77
300	7	Commonwealth Ave	78

301	6	Commonwealth Ave	78		379	99	Ocean Ave	94
302	6	Commonwealth Ave	78		380	99	Ocean Ave	94
303	6	Commonwealth Ave	78		381	4	Samoset Ave	95
304	3	Commonwealth Ave	78		382	6	Samoset Ave	95
305	14	Commonwealth Sq	78		383	12	Samoset Ave	95
306	13	Commonwealth Sq	78		384	14	Samoset Ave	95
307	12	Commonwealth Sq	79		385	14	Samoset Ave	95
308	25	Commonwealth Sq	79		386	14	Samoset Ave	95
309	34	Rock Ave	79		387	39	Narragansett Ave	97
310	28	Rock Ave	79		388	16	Samoset Ave	96
311	23	Rock Ave	79		389	26	Samoset Ave	98
312	22	Rock Ave	79		390	26	Samoset Ave	98
313	22	Rock Ave	80		391	27	Samoset Ave	96
314	14	Rock Ave	80		392	27	Samoset Ave	96
315	2	Hebron Ave	80		393	26	Samoset Ave	99
316	2	Hebron Ave	80		394	34	Samoset Ave	100
317	1	Hebron Ave	80		395	34	Samoset Ave	100
318	1	Hebron Ave	80		396	50	Narragansett Ave	100
319	12	Central Ave	80		397	42	Narragansett Ave	100
320	7	Central Ave	81		398	40	Narragansett Ave	100
322	8	Central Ave	81		399	40	Narragansett Ave	100
323	4	Central Ave	81		400	37	Narragansett Ave	100
324	4	Central Ave	81		401	38	Narragansett Ave	101
325	4	Central Ave	81		402	38	Narragansett Ave	101
326	2	Merrill Ave	82		403	34	Narragansett Ave	101
327	70	Lake Ave	82		404	32	Narragansett Ave	101
328	60	Lake Ave	82		405	31	Narragansett Ave	101
329	58	Lake Ave	82		406	28	Narragansett Ave	101
330	52	Lake Ave	82		407	28	Narragansett Ave	101
331	48	Lake Ave	82		408	22	Narragansett Ave	101
332	42	Lake Ave	83		409	12	Bayliss Ave	102
333	46	Lake Ave	84		410	22	Narragansett Ave	103
334	46	Lake Ave	84		411	20	Narragansett Ave	103
335	46	Lake Ave	84		412	21	Narragansett Ave	103
336	42	Lake Ave	84		413	19	Narragansett Ave	103
337	42	Lake Ave	83		414	18	Narragansett Ave	104
338	40	Lake Ave	84		415	16	Narragansett Ave	104
339	40	Lake Ave	85		416	15	Narragansett Ave	104
340	38	Lake Ave	85		417	15	Narragansett Ave	104
341	36	Lake Ave	85		418	10	Narragansett Ave	104
342	3	Siloam Ave	85		419	10	Narragansett Ave	105
343	3	Siloam Ave	85		420	8	Narragansett Ave	105
344	16	Siloam Ave	86		421	7	Narragansett Ave	105
345	4	Siloam Ave	87		422	6	Narragansett Ave	105
346	4	Siloam Ave	87		423	1	Narragansett Ave	106
347	6	Siloam Ave	87		424	1	Narragansett Ave	106
348	8	Siloam Ave	87		425	1	Narragansett Ave	106
349	8	Fourth Ave	89		426	7	Pequot Ave	106
350	8	Siloam Ave	88		427	8	Pequot Ave	106
351	12	Siloam Ave	88		428	10	Pequot Ave	106
352	12	Siloam Ave	88		429	12	Pequot Ave	107
353	13	Siloam Ave	88		430	15	Pequot Ave	107
354	15	Siloam Ave	88		431	19	Pequot Ave	107
355	17	Siloam Ave	88		432	23	Pequot Ave	107
356	19	Siloam Ave	90		433	23	Pequot Ave	107
357	19	Siloam Ave	90		434	27	Pequot Ave	107
358	29	Butler Ave	90		435	27	Pequot Ave	108
359	23	Ocean Ave	90		436	29	Pequot Ave	108
360	27	Ocean Ave	90		437	33	Pequot Ave	108
361	49	Ocean Ave	90		438	37	Pequot Ave	108
362	47	Ocean Ave	90		439	39	Pequot Ave	108
363	49	Ocean Ave	91		440	39	Pequot Ave	108
364	49	Ocean Ave	91		441	43	Pequot Ave	108
365	51	Ocean Ave	91		442	16	Pequot Ave	109
366	51	Ocean Ave	91		443	45	Pequot Ave	111
367	51	Ocean Ave	91		444	45	Pequot Ave	110
368	51	Ocean Ave	91		445	45	Pequot Ave	110
369	51	Ocean Ave	91		446	7	Tuckernuck Ave	110
370	51	Ocean Ave	92		447	45	Pequot Ave	110
371	53	Ocean Ave	93		448	49	Pequot Ave	112
372	53	Ocean Ave	93		449	53	Pequot Ave	112
373	8	Grove St	93		450	53	Pequot Ave	112
374	8	Grove St	93		451	57	Pequot Ave	112
375	79	Ocean Ave	94		452	59	Pequot Ave	112
376	89	Ocean Ave	94		453	60	Circuit Ave	112
377	93	Ocean Ave	94		454	30	Massasoit Ave	113
378	97	Ocean Ave	94		455	16	Massasoit Ave	112

456	12	Massasoit Ave	113
457	4	Massasoit Ave	113
458	81	Penacook Ave	112
459	74	Penacook Ave	112
460	74	Penacook Ave	113
461	77	Penacook Ave	113
462	71	Penacook Ave	113
463	56	Penacook Ave	112
464	52	Penacook Ave	113
465	50	Penacook Ave	113
466	3	Montgomery Sq	114
467	50	Penacook Ave	115
468	50	Penacook Ave	115
469	48	Penacook Ave	115
470	48	Penacook Ave	115
471	46	Penacook Ave	115
472	46	Penacook Ave	116
473	38	Penacook Ave	116
474	32	Penacook Ave	116
475	32	Penacook Ave	116
476	30	Penacook Ave	116
477	30	Penacook Ave	116
478	26	Penacook Ave	117
479	61	Ocean Ave	118
480	24	Penacook Ave	120
481	25	Penacook Ave	120
482	25	Penacook Ave	120
483	12	Penacook Ave	120
484	7	Penacook Ave	120
485	7	Penacook Ave	120
486	2	Naumkeag Ave	121
487	31	Nantucket Ave	121
488	16	Nantucket Ave	121
489	16	Nantucket Ave	121
490	8	Nantucket Ave	121
491	7	Tuckernuck Ave	121
492	9	Tuckernuck Ave	122
494	9	Tuckernuck Ave	123
495	11	Tuckernuck Ave	124
496	11	Tuckernuck Ave	124
497	11	Tuckernuck Ave	124
498	25	Tuckernuck Ave	124
499	33	Tuckernuck Ave	124
500	43	Tuckernuck Ave	124
501	45	Tuckernuck Ave	124
502	8	Vincent Park	125
503	48	Tuckernuck Ave	126
504	45	Tuckernuck Ave	127
505	48	Tuckernuck Ave	127
506	48	Tuckernuck Ave	127
507	48	Tuckernuck Ave	128
508	53	Tuckernuck Ave	128
509	55	Tuckernuck Ave	128
510	63	Tuckernuck Ave	128
511	71	Tuckernuck Ave	128
512	73	Tuckernuck Ave	128
513	7	Wamsutta Ave	128
514	11	Wamsutta Ave	129
515	15	Wamsutta Ave	129
516	4	Pocasset Ave	129
517	2	Pocasset Ave	129
518	37	Nashawena Park	129
519	20	Nashawena Park	129
520	55	Katama Ave	129
521	53	Katama Ave	129
522	23	Naushon Ave	130
523	23	Naushon Ave	130
524		Seaview & Nantucket	130
525		Seaview & Nantucket	130
526		Seaview & Samoset	130
527	54	Kennebec Ave	130
528	57	Kennebec Ave	130
529	46	Kennebec Ave	130
530	46	Kennebec Ave	130
531		School St	130
532	22	Pacific Ave	131
533	22	Pacific Ave	131
534	4	Pocasset Ave	133
535	21	Pacific Ave	132
536	18	Pacific Ave	132
537	146	Circuit Ave	132
538	148	Circuit Ave	132
539	150	Circuit Ave	132
540	Gazebo	Ocean Park	134
541	63	Circuit Ave	135
542	63	Circuit Ave	135
543	63	Circuit Ave	135
544	71	Circuit Ave	135
545	79	Circuit Ave	135
546	125	Circuit Ave	135
547	135	Circuit Ave	135
548	135	Circuit Ave	135
549	28	New York Ave	135
550	71	New York Ave	135
551	87	Ocean Ave	136
552	71	New York Ave	138
553	81	New York Ave	138
554	81	New York Ave	138
555	178	New York Ave	138
556	178	New York Ave	138
557	178	New York Ave	138
558	55	Ocean Ave	139
559	181	New York Ave	140
560	181	New York Ave	140
561	128	East Chop Dr	140
562	1	Brewster Ave	140
563	15	Wayland Ave	140
564	13	Wayland Ave	141
565	19	Beecher Park	141
566	19	Beecher Park	141
567	14	Beecher Park	141
568	8	Beecher Park	141
569	30	Pequot Ave	143
570	8	Dempster Park	142
571	8	Dempster Park	142
572	8	Dempster Park	142
573	18	John Wesley Ave	142
574	18	John Wesley Ave	142
575	14	John Wesley Ave	144
576	12	John Wesley Ave	144
577	12	John Wesley Ave	144
578	8	John Wesley Ave	144
579	8	John Wesley Ave	144
580	4	Rose Ave	144
581	49	Ocean Ave	145
582	52	Church Ave	146
583	62	Church Ave	146
584	62	Church Ave	146
585	62	Church Ave	146
586	29	Church Ave	146
587	29	Church Ave	146
588	81	Church Ave	146
589	7	Laurel Ave	147
590	10	Dorothy West Ave	147
591	10	Dorothy West Ave	147
592	16	Atlantic Ave	147
593		Seaview & Narragansett	148
594	16	Atlantic Ave	149
595	125	Munroe Ave	149
596	111	Munroe Ave	149
597	15	Lexington Ave	149
598	17	Plymouth Ave	149
599	17	Plymouth Ave	149
600	17	Plymouth Ave	149
601	9	Brunswick Ave	149
602		Beach Rd	148
603		Beach Rd	149
604		New York Ave	149
605	35	Allen Ave	150
606	17	Cottage Park	151

Address Index

Photo#	House #	Address	Page
278	26	Allen Ave	71
605	35	Allen Ave	150
592	16	Atlantic Ave	147
594	16	Atlantic Ave	149
223	1	Bayliss Ave	59
221	2	Bayliss Ave	59
222	2	Bayliss Ave	59
225	5	Bayliss Ave	60
224	6	Bayliss Ave	60
226	9	Bayliss Ave	60
227	9	Bayliss Ave	60
228	11	Bayliss Ave	60
229	11	Bayliss Ave	61
230	11	Bayliss Ave	61
231	12	Bayliss Ave	61
409	12	Bayliss Ave	102
602		Beach Rd	148
603		Beach Rd	149
568	8	Beecher Park	141
567	14	Beecher Park	141
565	19	Beecher Park	141
566	19	Beecher Park	141
562	1	Brewster Ave	140
601	9	Brunswick Ave	149
193	7	Butler Ave	51
194	7	Butler Ave	51
216	13	Butler Ave	58
197	19	Butler Ave	54
198	19	Butler Ave	54
199	19	Butler Ave	54
200	19	Butler Ave	54
358	29	Butler Ave	90
201	37	Butler Ave	54
202	39	Butler Ave	54
203	39	Butler Ave	54
323	4	Central Ave	81
324	4	Central Ave	81
325	4	Central Ave	81
320	7	Central Ave	81
322	8	Central Ave	81
319	12	Central Ave	80
272	3	Chapel Lane	69
273	3	Chapel Lane	69
275	3	Chapel Lane	71
586	29	Church Ave	146
587	29	Church Ave	146
582	52	Church Ave	146
583	62	Church Ave	146
584	62	Church Ave	146
585	62	Church Ave	146
588	81	Church Ave	146
453	60	Circuit Ave	112
541	63	Circuit Ave	135
542	63	Circuit Ave	135
543	63	Circuit Ave	135
544	71	Circuit Ave	135
545	79	Circuit Ave	135
546	125	Circuit Ave	135
547	135	Circuit Ave	135
548	135	Circuit Ave	135
537	146	Circuit Ave	132
538	148	Circuit Ave	132
539	150	Circuit Ave	132
114	2	Clinton Ave	37
115	8	Clinton Ave	37
175	9	Clinton Ave	49
116	10	Clinton Ave	39
117	10	Clinton Ave	38
118	10	Clinton Ave	38
119	12	Clinton Ave	38
120	12	Clinton Ave	38
102	13	Clinton Ave	34
121	14	Clinton Ave	40
122	14	Clinton Ave	41
123	14	Clinton Ave	41
124	14	Clinton Ave	41
125	18	Clinton Ave	41
173	19	Clinton Ave	49
126	22	Clinton Ave	41
127	22	Clinton Ave	41
172	23	Clinton Ave	49
171	25	Clinton Ave	48
128	26	Clinton Ave	42
129	26	Clinton Ave	42
130	30	Clinton Ave	42
131	30	Clinton Ave	42
132	30	Clinton Ave	42
169	31	Clinton Ave	48
170	31	Clinton Ave	48
168	35	Clinton Ave	48
133	36	Clinton Ave	42
134	38	Clinton Ave	43
135	38	Clinton Ave	43
136	42	Clinton Ave	43
165	45	Clinton Ave	48
166	45	Clinton Ave	48
137	46	Clinton Ave	43
138	46	Clinton Ave	43
162	49	Clinton Ave	46
164	49	Clinton Ave	48
139	50	Clinton Ave	43
140	50	Clinton Ave	43
141	50	Clinton Ave	43
143	57	Clinton Ave	45
144	59	Clinton Ave	45
145	62	Clinton Ave	45
146	62	Clinton Ave	45
147	62	Clinton Ave	45
148	63	Clinton Ave	45
149	66	Clinton Ave	45
176	5	Clinton Ave	49
174	13	Clinton Ave	49
167	35	Clinton Ave	48
304	3	Commonwealth Ave	78
301	6	Commonwealth Ave	78
302	6	Commonwealth Ave	78
303	6	Commonwealth Ave	78
299	7	Commonwealth Ave	77
300	7	Commonwealth Ave	78
298	10	Commonwealth Ave	77
61	12	Commonwealth Ave	23
297	12	Commonwealth Ave	77
290	14	Commonwealth Ave	74
292	17	Commonwealth Ave	76
293	17	Commonwealth Ave	77
294	17	Commonwealth Ave	77
295	17	Commonwealth Ave	77
296	17	Commonwealth Ave	77
285	18	Commonwealth Ave	74
286	18	Commonwealth Ave	74
287	21	Commonwealth Ave	74
288	21	Commonwealth Ave	74
289	21	Commonwealth Ave	74
280	24	Commonwealth Ave	72
281	24	Commonwealth Ave	73
282	24	Commonwealth Ave	73
283	24	Commonwealth Ave	73
284	24	Commonwealth Ave	73
279	26	Commonwealth Ave	71
307	12	Commonwealth Sq	79
306	13	Commonwealth Sq	78
305	14	Commonwealth Sq	78
308	25	Commonwealth Sq	79
232	1	Cottage Park	61
233	1	Cottage Park	61
234	1	Cottage Park	61
236	2	Cottage Park	63
237	7	Cottage Park	63
238	8	Cottage Park	63
239	11	Cottage Park	63
235	12	Cottage Park	62
240	12	Cottage Park	63
241	15	Cottage Park	63
242	16	Cottage Park	64
243	16	Cottage Park	64
606	17	Cottage Park	151
1	148	County Rd	7
570	8	Dempster Park	142
571	8	Dempster Park	142
572	8	Dempster Park	142
590	10	Dorothy West Ave	147
591	10	Dorothy West Ave	147
219	9	Dukes County Ave	58
217		Dukes County Ave	58
218		Dukes County Ave	58
561	128	East Chop Dr	140
244	6	Fisk Ave	64
245	8	Fisk Ave	64
246	8	Fisk Ave	64
207	1	Forest Circle	55
208	1	Forest Circle	55
209	3	Forest Circle	55
210	3	Forest Circle	55
211	4	Forest Circle	55
213	4	Forest Circle	58
214	4	Forest Circle	58
215	11	Forest Circle	58
206	15	Forest Circle	55
212	10 & 11	Forest Circle	56
349	8	Fourth Ave	89
276	10	Fourth Ave	71
274	15	Fourth Ave	70
277	15	Fourth Ave	71
373	8	Grove St	93
374	8	Grove St	93
317	1	Hebron Ave	80
318	1	Hebron Ave	80
315	2	Hebron Ave	80
316	2	Hebron Ave	80
578	8	John Wesley Ave	144
579	8	John Wesley Ave	144
576	12	John Wesley Ave	144
577	12	John Wesley Ave	144
575	14	John Wesley Ave	144
573	18	John Wesley Ave	142
574	18	John Wesley Ave	142
521	53	Katama Ave	129
520	55	Katama Ave	129
529	46	Kennebec Ave	130
530	46	Kennebec Ave	130
527	54	Kennebec Ave	130
528	57	Kennebec Ave	130
341	36	Lake Ave	85
340	38	Lake Ave	85
338	40	Lake Ave	84
339	40	Lake Ave	85
332	42	Lake Ave	83
336	42	Lake Ave	84
337	42	Lake Ave	83
333	46	Lake Ave	84
334	46	Lake Ave	84
335	46	Lake Ave	84
331	48	Lake Ave	82
330	52	Lake Ave	82
329	58	Lake Ave	82
328	60	Lake Ave	82
327	70	Lake Ave	82
589	7	Laurel Ave	147
597	15	Lexington Ave	149
457	4	Massasoit Ave	113
456	12	Massasoit Ave	113
455	16	Massasoit Ave	112
454	30	Massasoit Ave	113
326	2	Merrill Ave	82
466	3	Montgomery Sq	114

41	28	Trinity Park	16
42	30	Trinity Park	17
43	30	Trinity Park	17
3	31	Trinity Park	3
44	31	Trinity Park	17
45	34	Trinity Park	17
46	41	Trinity Park	17
47	42	Trinity Park	17
56	43	Trinity Park	22
57	44	Trinity Park	22
58	44	Trinity Park	22
59	44	Trinity Park	22
60	44	Trinity Park	22
142	44	Trinity Park	44
62	45	Trinity Park	24
63	45	Trinity Park	25
64	45	Trinity Park	25
65	47	Trinity Park	25
66	47	Trinity Park	25
258	47	Trinity Park	67
67	49	Trinity Park	25
68	52	Trinity Park	27
70	52	Trinity Park	27
69	53	Trinity Park	26
71	53	Trinity Park	27
72	54	Trinity Park	27
73	54	Trinity Park	27
74	54	Trinity Park	27
75	55	Trinity Park	27
77	55	Trinity Park	29
78	57	Trinity Park	29
79	57	Trinity Park	29
163	57	Trinity Park	47
80	58	Trinity Park	29
76	59	Trinity Park	28
81	59	Trinity Park	29
82	59	Trinity Park	29
84	60	Trinity Park	32
85	61	Trinity Park	32
86	62	Trinity Park	31
87	62	Trinity Park	31
88	62	Trinity Park	31
83	63	Trinity Park	31
89	63	Trinity Park	32
90	63	Trinity Park	32
91	65	Trinity Park	32
92	66	Trinity Park	32
93	66	Trinity Park	32
94	66	Trinity Park	32
95	67	Trinity Park	33
96	68	Trinity Park	33
97	68	Trinity Park	33
98	69	Trinity Park	33
220	69	Trinity Park	58
5	70	Trinity Park	8
6	70	Trinity Park	8
7	70	Trinity Park	8
8	70	Trinity Park	8
9	70	Trinity Park	9
99	72	Trinity Park	33
100	72	Trinity Park	33
101	74	Trinity Park	33
103	75	Trinity Park	34
104	75	Trinity Park	34
105	75	Trinity Park	34
106	75	Trinity Park	34
107	75	Trinity Park	34
108	75	Trinity Park	35
110	77	Trinity Park	37
111	79	Trinity Park	37
112	79	Trinity Park	37
113	80	Trinity Park	37
48	33+ 34	Trinity Park	18
51	Church	Trinity Park	21
52	Church	Trinity Park	21
53	Church	Trinity Park	21
54	Church	Trinity Park	21
49	Parish House	Trinity Park	20
50	Parish House	Trinity Park	20
55	Tabernacle	Trinity Park	21
446	7	Tuckernuck Ave	110
491	7	Tuckernuck Ave	121
492	9	Tuckernuck Ave	122
494	9	Tuckernuck Ave	123
495	11	Tuckernuck Ave	124
496	11	Tuckernuck Ave	124
497	11	Tuckernuck Ave	124
498	25	Tuckernuck Ave	124
499	33	Tuckernuck Ave	124
500	43	Tuckernuck Ave	124
501	45	Tuckernuck Ave	124
504	45	Tuckernuck Ave	127
503	48	Tuckernuck Ave	126
505	48	Tuckernuck Ave	127
506	48	Tuckernuck Ave	127
507	48	Tuckernuck Ave	128
508	53	Tuckernuck Ave	128
509	55	Tuckernuck Ave	128
510	63	Tuckernuck Ave	128
511	71	Tuckernuck Ave	128
512	73	Tuckernuck Ave	128
186	3	Victorian Park	51
185	5	Victorian Park	50
183	6	Victorian Park	50
184	6	Victorian Park	50
182	8	Victorian Park	50
181	11	Victorian Park	50
179	13	Victorian Park	50
180	13	Victorian Park	56
178	16	Victorian Park	50
177	19	Victorian Park	49
190	22	Victorian Park	51
191	22	Victorian Park	51
188	24	Victorian Park	51
189	24	Victorian Park	51
187	26	Victorian Park	51
192	27	Victorian Park	52
195	27	Victorian Park	52
196	28	Victorian Park	53
249	7	Vincent Park	64
502	8	Vincent Park	125
247	14	Vincent Park	64
248	14	Vincent Park	64
513	7	Wamsutta Ave	128
514	11	Wamsutta Ave	129
515	15	Wamsutta Ave	129
564	13	Wayland Ave	141
563	15	Wayland Ave	140
267	2	Wesleyan Grove	69
268	2	Wesleyan Grove	69
269	6	Wesleyan Grove	69
270	10	Wesleyan Grove	69
271	10	Wesleyan Grove	69
259	15	Wesleyan Grove	67
256	16	Wesleyan Grove	66
260	17	Wesleyan Grove	67
261	18	Wesleyan Grove	68
262	18	Wesleyan Grove	68
263	18	Wesleyan Grove	68
264	20	Wesleyan Grove	69
265	24	Wesleyan Grove	69
266	24	Wesleyan Grove	69
161	7	West Clinton Ave	46
160	16	West Clinton Ave	46
159	18	West Clinton Ave	46
157	21	West Clinton Ave	46
158	21	West Clinton Ave	46
155	22	West Clinton Ave	46
156	22	West Clinton Ave	46
153	23	West Clinton Ave	46
154	23	West Clinton Ave	46
152	24	West Clinton Ave	46
151	31	West Clinton Ave	45
150	35	West Clinton Ave	45